A BUSINESS OWNER'S GUIDE TO MAXIMIZE BUSINESS VALUATION

DARRELL AMY

CERTIFIED EXIT PLANNING ADVISOR

AUTHOR OF *REVENUE GROWTH ENGINE*

Disclaimer

This book is intended to provide general information only. Neither the author nor publisher provides any legal or other professional advice. If you need professional advice, you should seek advice from the appropriate licensed professional. This book does not provide complete information on the subject matter covered. This book is not intended to address specific requirements, either for an individual or an organization. This book is intended to be used only as a general guide and not as a sole source of information on the subject matter. While the author has undertaken diligent efforts to ensure accuracy, there is no guarantee of accuracy or of no errors, omissions or typographical errors. Any slights of people or organizations are unintentional. The author and publisher shall have no liability or responsibility to any person or entity and hereby disclaim all liability, including without limitation, liability for consequential damages regarding any claim, loss or damage that may be incurred, or alleged to have been incurred, directly or indirectly, arising out of the information provided in this book.

Published by: Convergence Consulting
ISBN: 978-1-7347743-3-7

“This book is dedicated to purpose-driven business owners who view their business as a platform to make a massive impact in the world.”

Table of Contents

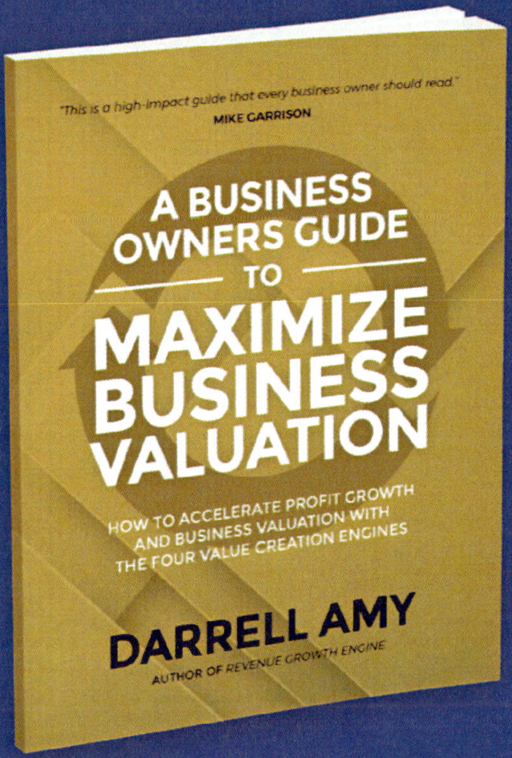

Who This Book Is For

This guide is written for purpose-driven business owners along with their financial advisors and leadership teams.

Purpose-driven business owners are leaders who are passionate about creating a great corporate culture, serving their customers, and giving back to the world.

This book provides an executive level overview of what it takes to create value in a way that maximizes the value of the business, creating freedom and options.

Why Focusing On Business Valuation Is Crucial

Many business owners focus on maximizing revenue and profit. However, the ultimate goal of every business owner should be to maximize value. The process of maximizing value lifts every other important metric in the business including revenue and profit.

When you focus on value you:

1 Unlock Wealth

By focusing on value there is a real possibility that you can 2X, 3X, and even 4X the value of your business. This unlocks wealth, proving attractive exit opportunities that could include a strategic sale where you take some or all of your chips off the table. This pile of resources can then be used to fuel generational wealth creation and high impact generosity.

2 Enable Legacy

Businesses with higher value are more sustainable. The engines that create value create an infrastructure of people and processes that empower the business to flourish. This helps ensure that the work you have done over decades can continue to thrive with new owners or a new generation of leadership.

3 Create Freedom

All of this gives you options. A highly valued business becomes less dependent on you. Outside the business you have the opportunity to spend more time with your family and friends. You finally even have the chance to travel without feeling like you have to check your email every 10 minutes. Inside the business you have the space, time, and budget to pursue growth through new ideas or acquisitions.

The challenge is that many business owners don't even measure that value of their business until they get ready to sell. As a result, they leave millions of dollars of value on the table. Ultimately, this value gets harvested by the person that buys the business.

The question to ask is, "Do I want to create and harvest value now, or do I want a future owner to reap the benefits of the foundation I have built?"

> "The ultimate goal of every business owner should be to **maximize value**—not just profit."

How Businesses Are Valued

Value is the amount a buyer is willing to offer a seller. The value of your business is dependent on both the quantity and the quality of the profits your business generates.

1

Quantity: EBITDA

This is the recast amount of EBITDA, (Earnings Before the deductions you take to reduce your taxable income: Interest, Taxes, Depreciation, and Amortization). Recasting means you add back expenses that a new owner might not incur such as excess compensation you might be taking or one-time expenses. This gives you "The Number"— the real cash flow stream from the business.

2

Quality: The Multiple

Every industry has a range of value that buyers are typically willing to pay. This gets expressed as a multiple of EBITDA. High quality businesses have lower risk to a buyer. Therefore, they are more likely to make an offer at a higher multiple. Medium quality businesses may command a multiple on the bottom end of the range. Low quality businesses that have not focused on value creation may ultimately have a multiple of zero. Sadly, this is a situation faced by many hard working business owners who focused on revenue and profit but neglected value.

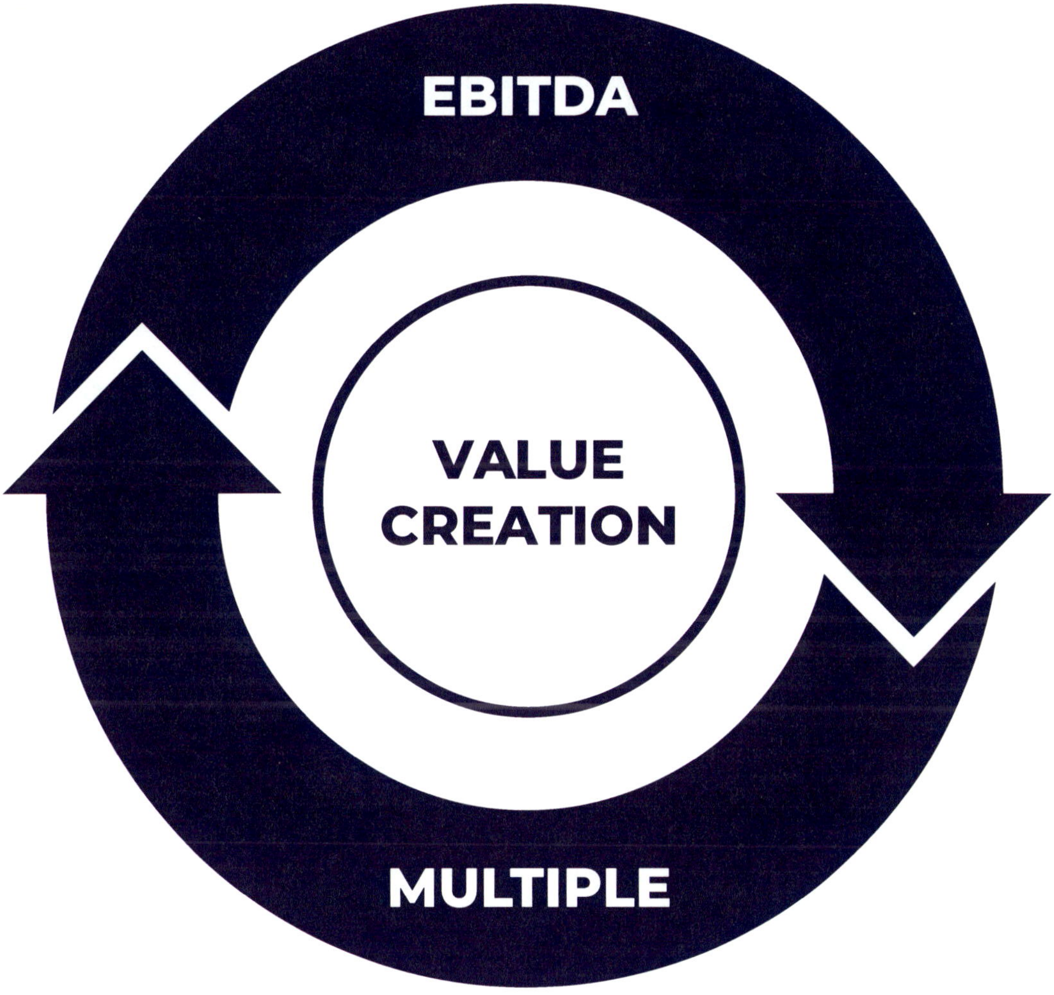

Only 40% of middle-market businesses have had a valuation done in the last 3 years

National Center for the Middle Market

What Is the Value of Your Business?

To estimate the value of your business, you need to know the current range of multiples on EBITDA in your industry. You also need to understand where your business would fall in that range of multiples.

Armed with this information you can discover two key numbers:

1

Current Value

Get a solid estimate of the market value of your business by multiplying your recast EBITDA by the multiple.

2

Best-In-Class Value

Find out what your business would be worth if you were able to achieve best-in-class profit margins. Multiply your revenue times the best-in-class profit margin for your business to find out what your EBITDA could be. Then, multiply the best-in-class EBITDA by the highest multiple in your industry. This will give you a best-in-class value for a company at your revenue level.

The difference between your current value and the best-in-class value represents your opportunity to grow value!

WHAT
GETS
MEASURED,
GETS
MANAGED

– Peter Drucker

How To 4X the Value of Your Business

Here is some great news: exponential value growth is possible!

Consider the following hypothetical example. A company has $20 million in revenue. After recasting their EBITDA, they are bringing 7% to the bottom line. Best-in-class companies are able to bring 15% to the bottom line. Industry multiples range from 4 to 8.

Let's say they were able to grow their revenue 10% year over year. With the right processes in place and an entrepreneurial culture they grew profits from 7% to 13%

	Present	Year 1	Year 2	Year 3
Revenue	$20M	$22M	$24.2M	$26.6M
EBITDA	7% $1.4M	9% $2.0	11% $2.7	13% $3.5
Multiple	4	5	6	7
Value	$5.6M	$10.0M	$16.2M	$24.5M

By growing revenue consistently while moving from below average toward best-in-class profits, this business increased its value from $5.6M to $24.5M in three years.

How could you do this? You need to maximize your four Value Creation Engines™.

The Four Value Creation Engines

When I fly overseas, I always feel more at ease in a plane that has multiple engines. My reasoning is that if one of the engines fails to perform, there are three more that will continue to keep us in the air. Two engines are okay, but I'd much rather have four!

When it comes to creating exponential value growth, you need four engines.

1 Revenue Growth: Powering consistent top-line growth.
2 Process Optimization: Driving efficiencies to maximize profitability.
3 Culture Development: Building an entrepreneurial culture.
4 Strategic Innovation: Becoming the recognized leader in your industry.

To drive value, each of these engines need to drive both quantity of profit (EBITDA) and quality of profits (Your Multiple).

Let's explore how each of these engines drive the value of your company.

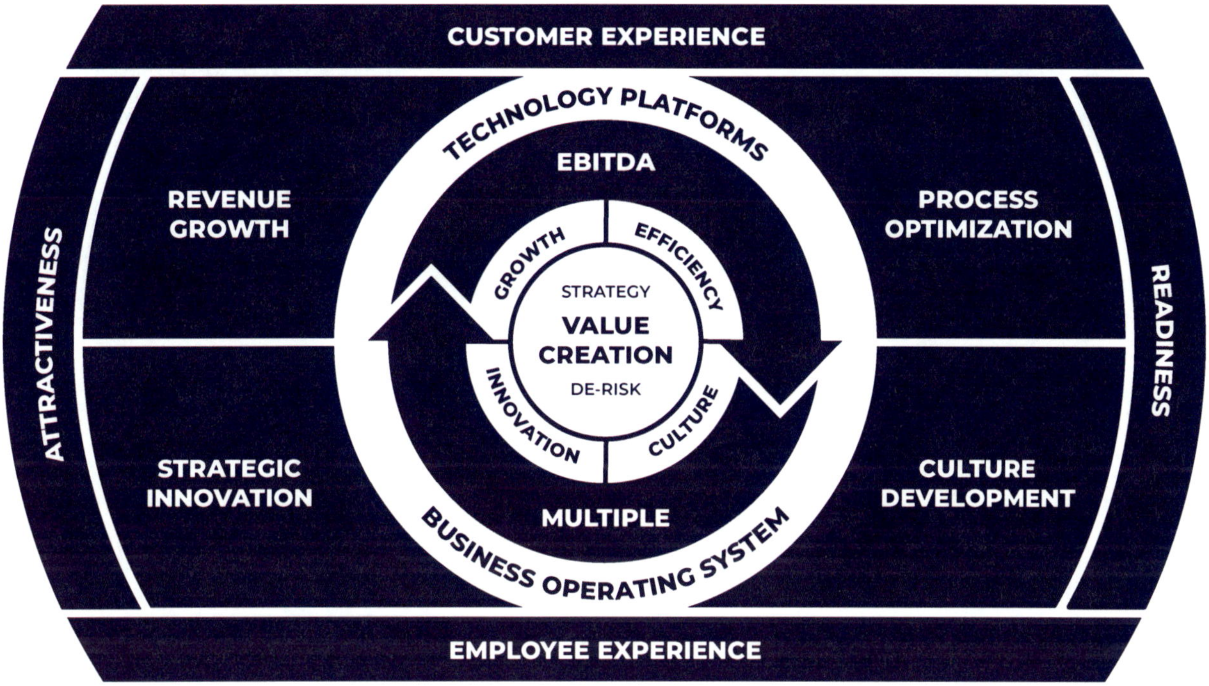

The Value Creation Engines Model

Revenue Growth Engine

Revenue fuels valuation. Companies with growing revenue attract a higher value than companies with flat growth. Revenue growth is a significant driver of company valuation because it reflects the company's ability to generate increasing income, which often signals overall business health, market demand, and future potential.

There are only two ways to grow revenue:

1 Net-New

You land (and keep) new customers.

2 Cross-Sell

You sell more to your current customers.

Most businesses are good at one or the other. Some are good at winning new deals. Others are great at harvesting the low-hanging fruit in their customer base. Companies that drive both net-new and cross-sell at the same time are able to experience exponential revenue growth.

The two core metrics for revenue growth are:

1 Number of Customers

This shows whether we are growing or shrinking the customer base.

2 Revenue per Customer

This reveals how effective we are at cross-selling more products and services.

When you get net-new and cross-sell growth working at the same time, you can create exponential revenue growth. Consider this example of a company that drives 12% growth in both net-new and cross-sell. This company doubles revenue in just three years.

	Growth Rate	Present	Year 1	Year 2	Year 3
Net-New (Number of Customers)	12%	1,000	1,120	1,254	1,404
Cross-Sell (Revenue per Customer)	12%	$10,000	$11,200	$12,540	$14,040
Total Revenue		$10.0M	$12.5M	$15.7M	$19.7M

What a High-Performance Revenue Growth Engine Looks Like

- Marketing and sales work together to consistently drive net-new and cross-sell revenue.
- Marketing and sales processes are fully aligned.
- Teams work together to continually improve the processes.
- The message resonates with ideal clients.
- The brand makes the company look and feel like the category leader.
- The company is not overly dependent on one salesperson or customer.
- There is a scorecard which is updated weekly with meaningful leading indicators.

> *Companies with effective net-new and cross-sell strategies can achieve **exponential revenue growth.***

Process Optimization Engine

Boil a business down to its most basic components and you will find two things: people and processes. While revenue is the fuel of business, processes are like the gears. When they work well together, the business can accelerate. Streamlined operations make the business more attractive to investors or buyers, who value predictability, scalability, and resilience.

Processes are a series of steps for a repeated outcome. They are the actions that your business does over and over and over again. These need to be done consistently across your team.

There are two issues related to processes:

1 Not Documented

With no documented processes you find that everyone is doing their own thing. This makes it very hard to ensure quality, troubleshoot problems, and onboard new employees. This would be especially concerning to a potential buyer.

2 Not Optimized

While some companies do have documented processes, many of them fail to continually improve the processes. The documented processes sit on the shelf. Smart companies drive value by continually analyzing their processes looking for ways to improve productivity, reduce bottlenecks, and cut waste. They also look for ways to leverage technology to automate processes.

While the core metric for revenue growth is Revenue per Customer, the core metric for process optimization is Revenue per Employee. As you optimize your processes, you build efficiencies that continually increase Revenue per Employee.

What a High-Performance Process Optimization Engine Looks Like

- Processes are documented in a way that a new employee could get up to speed quickly.
- Everyone does the same thing the same way.
- Processes are continually improved.
- Processes leverage automation to drive efficiency.
- Checklists and dashboards ensure the processes are on track.
- Customer satisfaction is measured and tracked.

> *Streamlined operations make the business **more attractive to buyers** who value predictability, scalability, and resilience.*

Culture Development Engine

Peter Drucker famously said, "Culture eats strategy for breakfast." Every business has a culture. Company culture plays a crucial role in determining the value of a business, as it impacts employee engagement, customer satisfaction, productivity, and risk management. A strong, positive culture can make a company more attractive to investors and acquirers because it signals stability, resilience, and long-term potential.

For some businesses, the culture happens by accident. In high-value businesses, culture happens intentionally.

The best type of culture is an entrepreneurial culture. Everyone understands the goal of growing value. Employees not only work IN the business, they also have a role in working ON the business. Employee engagement increases as they collaborate on teams aimed at creating value.

All of these corporate characteristics are measured. While customers provide measurable feedback through tools like a Net Promoter Score, employees provide measurable feedback on their experience and the overall culture.

What a High-Performance Culture Development Engine Looks Like

- Leadership communicates and lives the core values.
- Documented OKRs[1] for the company, departments, and individuals.
- Everyone celebrates achievements and promotions.
- Each role has a clear job description with a documented career growth path.
- There are consistent touchpoints between leaders and their direct reports.
- Leadership has developed a written succession plan for key leadership positions.
- Each employee has a plan and budget for skill development.
- Employee engagement is measured and tracked.

> ***A high-performance culture*** *isn't accidental; it's intentionally crafted and nurtured.*

Strategic Innovation Engine

Businesses that want to accelerate value growth should pay attention to innovation. Getting strategic about innovation creates value by unlocking new streams of revenue while positioning the company as a true leader in the marketplace.

While every Fortune 500 company has an innovation initiative, the majority of mid-market companies fail to consistently innovate. As a result, they not only miss potential opportunities, they also become vulnerable to savvy competitors.

Strategic Innovation is the process of creating value for ideal clients by developing, piloting, and packaging breakthrough products, services, and experience to create transformation and build competitive advantage. While the Process Optimization Engine is innovating to increase efficiency, the Strategic Innovation Engine works to create new products and services to serve emerging and existing markets.

The key metric for Strategic Innovation is revenue growth attributed to new products.

What a High-Performance Strategic Innovation Engine Looks Like

A cross-functional team works on a quarterly cadence to come up with new ideas.

- Regular rollouts of new or enhanced products and services occur.
- Revenue and profit growth can be attributed to new offerings.
- Expansion flows into new customer groups, industries, or markets.
- A process is documented to pilot and optimize new ideas.
- A wall of innovation features successful innovation.
- Recognition comes as a category leader in your industry.

Strategic innovation ***unlocks new revenue streams*** *and positions your company as* ***an industry leader.***

Your Onboard Computer

All of today's high-performance automobiles have onboard computers. To maximize the value of your business, you need two onboard computers:

Business Operating System

Just as your computer and phone have operating systems that guide how everything works together, every business needs an operating system. This is a shared set of practices for how the company will set goals, achieve them, and measure success. And in the same way that you can run a computer on Windows, Mac, or Linux, you can run a business on operating systems like EOS®, Scaling Up Business System, or Pinnacle. Businesses with a reliable operating system are able to drive consistent results while also working to improve the overall business.

> *"A reliable business operating system and updated technology are essential to maximize valuation."*

Technology Platforms

The technology that your business uses can also have a large impact on valuation. The wrong technology slows things down, draining productivity and profits. The right technology properly implemented and used can turbocharge valuation. Since technology continues to evolve, especially with the latest advances in Artificial Intelligence, companies need to continually evaluate ways to leverage technology to drive revenue and maximize profits.

Just as modern vehicles rely on onboard computers to optimize performance, businesses need both a solid operating system and up-to-date technology platforms to maximize their valuation. A reliable business operating system aligns goals, streamlines processes, and fosters consistent growth, while the right technology enhances productivity, scales efficiency, and adapts to advancements like artificial intelligence. Together, these two «onboard computers» are essential for driving your business toward increased profitability, competitive advantage, and long-term value.

The Outputs

A powerful engine creates horsepower and torque that provide acceleration. My newest car has a display that not only shows the speed, it also shows horsepower and torque as I accelerate onto the freeway.

Your Value Creation Engines creates acceleration in two ways:

1 Horsepower

Customer Experience

What's it like to be your customer? Companies like Chic-fil-A® and Amazon have elevated customer expectations by fanatically improving customer experience. Improving your customer experience leads to loyal customers who buy more. This increases the value of your company.

Employee Experience

What's it like to be an employee at your company? One of the biggest drains of profitability is employee turnover. Developing your culture while fostering strategic innovation helps create an experience that attracts and retains top talent. This drives increased profits and increased value.

2 Torque

Readiness to Sell

If someone offered to buy your company today, would it be ready to hand off? Or, would the buyer make you stay onboard as an owner for several years to complete the handoff? A business with a powerful Value Creation Engine should be ready to handoff.

Attractiveness to a Buyer

Would a buyer get excited about buying your business? An attractive business is the type of business a buyer looks at and says, "I wish all my businesses looked like this!" A business that is attractive is able to bring in offers from strategic buyers who may be willing to pay a premium for the business outside of the normal range of value.

> *An attractive business is the type a buyer looks at and says, 'I wish all my businesses looked like this!*

81% of business owners who sold their business wish they had spent more time preparing

UBS Research, 2023

Fall In Love With Your Business Again

There's something special about sliding into the driver's seat of a high-performance vehicle. As you start the engine you hear an inviting rumble. Leaning into the gas pedal you feel the acceleration push you back into your seat. Corners become a challenge to see how well the car will grip the road.

Once you experience this, you find it hard to get excited to drive a car with less horsepower and torque. In the same way, once you begin to experience the feeling of value creation you won't want to go back.

Many business owners start focusing on value creation in the months leading up to a planned sale. There are two problems with this. First, you can only accelerate so much in a few months. No wonder a recent survey found that 81% of owners who sold their business wished they had spent more time preparing.[2]

The second problem with waiting to start the value creation process is that over 50% of exits are unplanned. The unfortunate events of death, disability, divorce, and disagreement lead many owners to need to sell their businesses quickly. Wise business owners who have prepared by creating value are able to harvest wealth, while unprepared business owners often sell (or liquidate) at a much lower value than they had hoped for.

When you ***experience value creation,*** *you'll find it hard to go back to business as usual.*

"If you do
what you have
always done,
you will get
what you have
always got."

– Henry Ford

Improve Your Engines

To accelerate value you need to begin improving your engines. This is a three step process you can remember with the acronym MPG.

Measure

You need to know the current market value of your business. The best way to do this is to compare your business to other recent transactions in your industry. The way this works is simple:

1. First, determine the market value of your business by understanding the range of multiples in your market along with what best-in-class profitability looks like. This will help us understand what the best-in-class business value looks like, giving you an idea of what could be possible with high-performance Value Creation Engines.
2. Next, recast your EBITDA to get to the Real Number. This is the profitability of your business after factoring out excess compensation and rents, one-time disbursements , and other discretionary expenses that a new owner would not incur.
3. The next step is to determine where your business would fall

on the range of multiples. Do this by taking a deep dive into each component of your Value Creation Engines with the goal of benchmarking the Readiness and Attractiveness of the business.

4. Finally, find out what the best-in-class profit margins are in your industry. Multiply this by your revenue to determine what best-in-class profit could look like for you. Then, multiply the best-in-class profit by the top industry multiple to get an understanding of the potential value of your business.

A Value Creation Engines Guide can help you through these steps to get an accurate estimate of the value of your business along with the potential value. This allows you to get an accurate picture of the current market value of your business along with a vision for what it could be worth.

Plan

The next step is to build an actionable Value Creation Plan. Based on your timeframe, we can collaborate with you and your financial advisor to align your business goals with your personal goals. Then, we work with you and your leadership team to build an actionable Value Creation Plan to maximize each of your Value Creation Engines.

Grow

Now it's time to get to work. Plans must turn quickly into action. At Value Creation Engines our motto is, "Let's Get Growing!"

We build momentum by working in cross-functional team of employees working on the Value Creation Engines. Why employees?

Getting your team engaged in working ON the business drives engagement. It creates an entrepreneurial culture while also building a pipeline of future leaders.

Smaller companies may have one Value Creation Council that works on all four engines over time. Larger companies that want to accelerate faster may stand up cross-functional teams in each of the four value creation areas: Revenue Growth, Process Optimization, Culture Development, and Strategic Innovation.

These teams work in 90-day sprints. Each quarter they invest half a day reviewing progress and planning the next quarter. They set OKRs for the next quarter along with milestones. During the quarter the team meets monthly to discuss progress and solve problems.

Each quarter builds on the previous quarter, building momentum in each of the four value creation engines.

Every success story is a tale of constant adaption, revision, and change.

–Richard Branson

The Results

The results of focusing on value creation are fantastic! In addition to creating value, this process unleashes:

1. More resources as revenue and profits grow
2. Higher employee engagement
3. Increased customer satisfaction
4. An entrepreneurial culture

In addition to all these results, the greatest benefits are freedom and options. As an owner, you become free to pursue their passions inside and outside the business. More and more attractive options emerge to secure your future with an intentional exit plan based on your goals.

This is what can happen when you focus on creating value by upgrading your Value Creation Engines.

Step one is to find out what your business is worth right now along with what it could be worth. To take this important first step visit measure.valuecreationengines.com for a confidential consultation.

Unlock the potential of your business and start maximizing your value today. Discover how to leverage the Four Value Creation Engines to build a business that delivers freedom, options, and lasting legacy. Schedule a free, confidential valuation consultation to get an estimate of your business›s current worth, along with insights on how to increase its valuation. Our team is here to guide you on the path to exponential growth and value creation.

ABOUT VALUE CREATION ENGINES

Value Creation Engines exists to help purpose-driven business owners multiply their value so they can maximize their impact.

We partner with owners of established businesses and their financial advisors to accelerate value in a way that creates options and freedom.

Our BHAG (Big, Holy, Audacious Goal) is to help 10,000 business owners multiply their value to create $100 billion in new value and $10 billion in new giving.

ABOUT DARRELL AMY

Darrell is a value creation advisor passionate about helping purpose-driven business owners make an impact. Based on over three decades serving hundreds of mid-market businesses, Darrell devotes his experience to creating models and frameworks to help businesses maximize their value.

He is the author of the bestseller *Revenue Growth Engine.* He is a regular speaker at business events and enjoys sharing growth ideas on business podcasts.

Darrell is a Certified Exit Planning Advisor (CEPA). This ensures that the models and frameworks that the Value Creation Engines team creates and implements align with business owners and their financial advisors as they create personal goals and financial plans.

THE MPG PROCESS TO CREATE VALUE

1 MEASURE

You get an accurate estimate of the current and potential value of your business based on current industry multiples and a detailed assessment of your busines

2 PLAN

In partnership with your financial advisor, we co-develop a comprehensive Value Creation Plan so you can hit your personal and business goals.

3 GROW

We guide you and your Value Creation Team(s) through executing 90-day sprints to maximize enterprise value while reducing risk.

Learn more at **www.valuecreationengines.com**

Other Books By DARRELL AMY

Darrell Amy's first book, *Revenue Growth Engine*, provides a powerful roadmap to synchronize your sales and marketing efforts to fuel sustainable growth. Ideal for business owners and leaders, *Revenue Growth Engine* lays out actionable strategies and tools that align revenue-generating teams to drive consistent, scalable growth. Packed with insights from Darrell›s 20+ years of experience, this book offers proven frameworks to unlock untapped revenue potential and build a robust growth engine.

End Notes:

1 Objectives and Key Results

2 UBS Reasearch: https://www.ubs.com/us/en/wealth-management/who-we-serve/specialized-advice/business-owners/planning-a-business-sale.html

Notes and Action Items

Notes and Action Items